Grammar

Grade 4

Reading and writing are the cornerstones of education. The basics of these skills include reading comprehension and a working knowledge of grammar and spelling. Language class, in which students develop their foundation of English, should be an enjoyable, educational experience for all students. This is possible, however, only if students are conscious of steady progress in their written language, and if they understand what they are doing.

This *Grammar Grade 4* book is part of a *Basics First* series that has been designed to help students succeed in grammar usage. The activities were created to help students feel confident about their grammar skills and help them understand the steps involved in learning these skills.

The pages have been arranged in an easy-to-follow format. This format allows the teacher to choose from a variety of fourth-grade grammar skills that are presented in an interesting, relevant, and age-appropriate manner. Each skill begins with rules. These rules are followed by intensive practice with interesting information. The skills included are those that every fourth-grade student should possess in order to express himself or herself confidently in spoken and written English.

With more emphasis being placed on the traditional basic subjects, it is easy to understand the vital role grammar plays in everyone's life. It has become clear how important the teaching of grammar is in helping students to become confident in their English usage.

This book can be used alone or as an integral part of any language program. It can also be used in conjunction with literature-based programs to provide students with the benefits of a well-rounded English language education.

The Subject Is Fun!

Name _____

The **subject** of a sentence tells whom or what the sentence is about.

Underline the subject of each sentence by asking yourself whom or what the sentence is about.

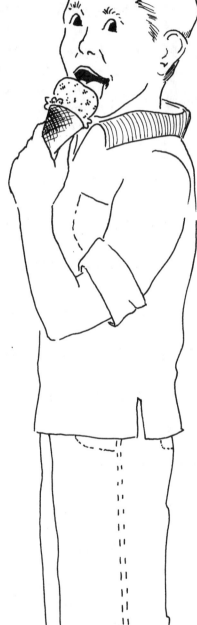

1. Peter likes strawberry ice cream.

2. A chocolate malt costs $3.00.

3. Peter bought the cool treat on his way home from school.

4. Peter worked in a bike shop near his home.

5. The woman in the gray car is his mother.

6. She has three sons and one daughter.

7. Her sister's name is Angie.

8. Michelle thinks Jim is very funny.

9. The rollerblades were left out all night.

10. Bike riding is popular year-round in California.

11. San Diego has more bike paths than St. Louis.

12. The boys live in an apartment near the beach.

13. The man in the green car is my father.

14. Mr. Farmer drove his tractor into my father's new car.

15. Jogging in Queeny Park can be very relaxing.

Try This! Write five sentences containing subjects relating to school. Underline the subjects.

2

FS-30043 Grammar

Take Action

Name _____

The **predicate** tells what the subject does or is.
The **complete predicate** is the verb along with its modifiers.
Underline the complete predicate in each sentence.

1. The boy with the black skateboard is his best friend.

2. All of Michael's friends have computers at home.

3. Harriet drove her van to school.

4. Michael goes to that newly built school.

5. He takes computer classes after school.

6. Anne's favorite outdoor sport is horseback riding.

7. Learning to use the computer was not very hard for him.

8. Michael's friend Anne takes dancing lessons on Saturdays.

9. These two friends worked on their science project together.

10. She teaches fourth grade at Washington Elementary School.

When dinosaurs roamed

Circle each verb in the sentences above. Write them in alphabetical order on the lines below.

1. _____   6. _____

2. _____   7. _____

3. _____   8. _____

4. _____   9. _____

5. _____   10. _____

Try This! Write directions telling how to do something. Underline the complete predicates in your directions.

Take a Holiday!

Name _____

The **complete subject** is all the words that tell who or what a sentence is about.
The **complete predicate** is all the words that tell what the subject is or does.

Draw a diagonal line between the complete subject and complete predicate in the sentences below.

1. On Labor Day, we go to the lake for the last time of the year.

2. Our school has the Halloween Party at the end of the day.

3. Everyone will bring a dish of food for Thanksgiving dinner.

4. Hanukkah is sometimes called the Feast of Lights.

5. The Jennings' Christmas tree was covered with candy.

6. I would like to be in New York on New Year's Day.

7. My father gave my mother an enormous Valentine last year.

8. Patrick and his sister Megan led the St. Paddy's Day parade.

9. The Easter Egg Hunt is held on the front lawn of the White House.

10. My family celebrates Passover with many delicious foods.

11. Jim, Mike, and Peter were all born in May.

12. Our school will close one week after Memorial Day.

13. The Fourth of July is always noisy around our neighborhood.

14. My hometown of St. Louis is always hot and humid in August.

Try This! In the sentences above, underline the simple subject and circle the simple predicate.

4

Something's Missing

Name _____

Complete the sentences below by adding a complete subject.
Put two lines under the simple subject and one line under the complete subject.

1. ____Our dog____ chewed my homework .

2. _____ were as big as my feet.

3. _____ roared at us.

4. _____ are far away from here.

5. _____ were full of scales.

6. _____ pulled their team
jerseys over their heads before going on the field.

7. _____ has not heard if they are going on a field trip next Tuesday.

8. _____ climbed to the top of the mountain.

9. _____ packed warm clothing before their trip to Alaska.

10. _____ bought new swimsuits for the spring break in Florida.

 **Try This!** On the back of this page, write three sentences about your city. Circle the simple subjects and underline the complete subjects.

5

FS-30043 Grammar

Off to the Cinema

Name _____

Complete the sentences below by writing a complete predicate. Circle the verb and underline the complete predicate.

1. One day, Mary (rode) her bicycle to the park.

2. Her bicycle _____

3. Mary and Jennifer _____

4. After a while, Mike _____

5. His front bicycle tire _____

6. For lunch, they _____

7. The whole group _____

8. The movie theater _____

9. The popcorn _____

10. Some people _____

11. That movie _____

12. Most of the audience _____

13. Our jeep _____

14. The cold wind _____

15. Mary, Jennifer, and Mike _____

Try This! Draw a box around the simple subject in each sentence.

Looking Closer

Name _____

There are eight parts of speech: **nouns**, **pronouns**, **adjectives**, **verbs**, **adverbs**, **prepositions**, **conjunctions**, and **interjections**. These are labels given to words in order to classify their relationship to the other words in the sentence. The way a word is used in a sentence determines its part of speech.

Find the eight parts of speech in the word find below. Write them on the proper line beneath the word find.

S	L	R	O	P	A	W	E	L	L	I
C	F	T	V	E	R	B	P	A	S	N
A	O	A	D	W	T	L	R	T	D	T
D	E	N	P	I	N	D	E	O	G	E
J	P	O	J	S	O	E	P	I	E	R
E	W	A	L	U	U	P	O	N	A	J
C	A	D	J	P	N	R	S	W	L	E
T	L	V	K	E	R	C	I	S	E	C
I	K	E	D	L	P	N	T	T	W	T
V	D	R	V	Q	T	I	I	I	T	I
E	F	B	N	O	I	N	O	L	O	O
A	P	G	M	P	R	O	N	O	U	N

_ _ _ r _ _ _ _ _

_ _ _ o _ _ _ _ _ _ _ _ _

_ _ d _ _ _ _ _ _ _ _

_ _ _ _ _ j _ _ _ _ _ _ _

_ _ _ p _ _ _ _ _ _

_ _ _ t _ _ _ _ _ _ _ _

_ o _ _ _ _

_ u _ _ _ _ _ _

Try This! Use your dictionary and write the abbreviation for each part of speech. Then see if you can write an example of each part of speech.

7

Sights to See

Name _____

A **noun** names a person, place, or thing.

A **common noun** denotes one of a class of persons, places, or things.

A **proper noun** names a particular person, place, or thing and begins with a capital letter.

Choose your own proper and common noun for each sentence.

1. __Washington__ is the __capital__ of the United States.
   proper   common

2. Last summer, _____ went there on her _____.
   proper   common

3. On her second day in Washington, _____ and her_____ met
   proper   common
   the President.

4. They asked President _____ if his _____ was at home.
   proper   common

5. After _____, the group visited the _____ .
   common   proper

6. The Vietnam Veterans Memorial is dedicated to the _____ who fought in
   common
   the _____.
   proper

7. Visitors experience feelings of wonder when they see the Lincoln Memorial where the
   _____ of Abraham _____ is overwhelming.
   common   proper

8. Our first president, _____ chose the exact spot for the
   proper
   _____ of Washington in 1791.
   common

⭐ **Try This!** Write five common nouns with a proper noun that would be in the same class. Then make a list of ten proper nouns relating to your school.

Noun Nonsense

Nouns

Name _____

Circle the nouns in each sentence. Write *C* above it if it is common and *P* if it is proper.

1. Bubbly Barbara bounced her basketball against the backboard.

2. Cute Carl caught a catastrophic cold in Canada.

3. Dreary Dorothy decided to drop dancing.

4. Every early Easter, Eugene dyes the eggs.

5. Finding Frank flat on his face fascinated Frances.

6. George gave Gracie a golden goose for her graduation.

7. Have you had healthy hamburgers at home lately?

8. Ice cream ignites indigestion in Ian's in-laws.

9. Justin just jerked jellybeans gently from his jacket.

10. Keeping Karen quiet in kindergarten causes the kangaroo to kick.

11. Lucy lost lots of laughs lingering in the lunchroom line.

12. Many motor mouths manage to mention too many memories.

13. Notice Nancy nudging Norman near his neck.

14. Often on October outings, Otto offers oranges to officers.

15. Patricia practically punched Paul off the porch.

16. Quiet Quentin quickly quartered the quilt.

Try This! On the back of this page, write three of your own nonsense sentences and circle the nouns.

© Frank Schaffer Publications, Inc.

9

FS-30043 Grammar

Watch for Bears

Name _____

Proper nouns name a particular person, place, or thing. They begin with capital letters.
Complete the board below by writing four proper nouns for each common noun.

people	George Washington			
stores				
teams				
streets				
months				
schools				
national parks				
countries				

Try This! Write a proper noun for each of these common nouns: a car, your mom, a tourist attraction, a movie theater. Include them in a story.

⟨10⟩   FS-30043 Grammar

Compute This!

Name _____

A noun is a **possessive noun** when it shows possession or ownership.

In order to show that a singular noun owns something, you must write the noun and add *'s*.

 Example

THE SCREEN OF THE COMPUTER

THE COMPUTER'S SCREEN

Show that each of the underlined nouns owns something by writing it as a possessive.

1. the computer of <u>Angie</u> _____

2. the stethoscope of the <u>doctor</u> _____

3. the land of the <u>farmer</u> _____

4. the painting of the <u>artist</u> _____

5. the pupils of the <u>teacher</u> _____

6. the mitt of the <u>catcher</u> _____

7. the name of the <u>astronaut</u> _____

8. the water of the <u>lake</u> _____

9. the horse of <u>Kathy</u> _____

10. the hat of <u>Mr. Lincoln</u> _____

 **Try This!** Write three sentences about your family. Show that someone owns something in each sentence. Use possessive nouns.

FS-30043 Grammar

Keeping Your Balance

Name _____

Pronouns take the place of nouns.

Personal pronouns name the speaker, the person spoken to, or the person or thing spoken of. They are:

Singular	Plural
I, my, mine	we, our, ours, us
he, his, him	you, your, yours
she, her, hers	they, them,
you, your, yours	their, theirs
it, its	

Write seven sentences using at least two personal pronouns in each sentence. Circle the pronouns.

1. _____

2. _____

3. _____

4. _____

5. _____

6. _____

7. _____

Try This! Go back to your sentences and write an appropriate noun above each pronoun.

FS-30043 Grammar

Biking Business

Name _____

Pronouns take the place of nouns.

Replace the pronouns in each sentence with a common or proper noun.

1. He kept the bicycle in the garage.

2. It came with extra tires.

3. Do you think she can bike five miles?

4. It is my favorite kind of bicycle.

5. They ride the tandem bicycle on the Katy Trail.

6. After school, we will ride our dirt bikes to the park.

7. It closes at six o'clock.

8. Dad put them on a carrier attached to the trunk.

9. Mine has a holder for a bottle of water.

10. The black one is hers.

11. Mom came with us to the bike-a-thon.

12. The jackets found on the side of the road are theirs.

13. Yours are in your locker at school.

14. Its tire is flat.

15. I think biking is the best exercise for us.

 **Try This!** On the back of this page, write 15 pronouns.

FS-30043 Grammar

There, Their!

Name _____

If you need a possessive pronoun, use **their**.

Example   *Their* skates were on the steps.

If you need to tell where, use **there**.

Example   The skates are *there*.

There are the skates.

Write *their* or *there* in the blanks in the sentences below.

1. _____ is the President of the United States.

2. It is _____ country that we wish to visit.

3. _____ ambassador was late for the dinner.

4. Put the trophy over _____.

5. Judith and Emily put _____ coats over _____.

6. _____ are five Americans on the committee.

7. _____ flag is the one on the right.

8. The new computers will be set up over _____.

9. England and France sent _____ teams _____.

10. Would you like to go _____?

11. _____ food is ready. It's over _____.

12. Will they go _____ with me if I bring _____ books?

13. Over _____ is where I saw the puppy.

Try This!   *There* and *their* are homophones. Write 10 pairs of homophones.

14

Pecos Bill

Name _____

A **verb** expresses action or indicates state of being.

A **verb phrase** is the verb with the helping words.

Example   *The student should have been working.*

Working is the verb.
Should have been working is the verb phrase.

In the following story, circle the verbs and underline the verb phrases.

When Pecos Bill was a baby, he was as tough as a pine knot. He teethed on horseshoes instead of teething rings and played with grizzly bears instead of teddy bears. He could have grown up fine in Texas but one day, his pappy felt it was getting too crowded. So Bill's folks loaded their 15 kids and all their stuff and started west.

As they moved across western Texas, the scorching heat nearly drove them all crazy. Little Bill got so hot that he started bugging his 14 brothers and sisters until all 15 kids were going at it tooth and nail. They could have turned Baby Bill into catfish bait, but he fell out of the wagon and landed smack on the sun-blazing desert.

The others had been fighting so long that they didn't notice the baby missing until they pulled into camp for the night.

Now Bill just sat there in the dirt watching an old coyote walk up to him and sniff him all over.

Bill said the only words he knew, "Goo-goo", which means "Glad to meet you" in coyote. Of course, the old coyote thought he had found a friend, so he picked Bill up and carried him back to his den.

Try This!   Write a paragraph about another legendary figure. Circle the verbs and underline at least two verb phrases.

15

Sharp Eyes

Name _____

Linking verbs link the subject to another word in the predicate. They help tell us what the subject is. Here are some common linking verbs:

is	am	are	was	were	turns
turn	stands	be	been	being	will
did	do	becomes	grows	remains	looks
seems	sounds	tastes	appears	feels	smells

Find the 24 linking verbs listed above in the word find below.

```
L  I  L  S  M  E  L  L  S  M  I  S  O  G  R
O  R  E  I  J  K  E  D  I  D  A  E  R  T  E
O  W  S  Q  R  S  T  E  R  U  P  O  L  G  M
K  L  O  Z  T  A  O  A  G  O  W  O  T  F  A
S  T  U  A  F  E  E  L  S  S  F  P  U  D  I
P  J  N  O  P  Q  O  G  U  T  V  S  R  G  N
E  E  D  Z  A  B  L  K  E  R  E  C  N  Y  S
A  Y  S  R  A  E  P  P  A  E  B  S  K  A  T
T  U  R  L  R  P  T  W  M  A  O  P  R  I  A
U  B  A  D  O  U  E  S  L  P  A  E  W  M  S
L  E  M  O  E  S  R  X  R  O  C  A  L  O  T
W  I  L  L  J  A  V  B  E  C  O  M  E  S  A
E  N  O  M  L  W  S  E  D  A  T  K  G  L  N
R  G  O  W  O  H  D  E  R  E  W  I  T  Z  D
S  N  R  U  T  G  L  N  N  O  P  L  S  V  S
```

Try This! On the back of this page, list 20 linking verbs. Using all 20 linking verbs, write a story about a summer vacation you would like to take.

FS-30043 Grammar

Our Neighborhood

Name _____

Underline the **linking verb** twice and draw an arrow above the subject to the word that renames or describes the subject.

 Example Mom sounds happy.

James is a biker.

1. Joe is a neighbor.

2. He usually seems happy.

3. I am pleased.

4. Joe became a boxer.

5. Karen is his wife.

6. She was a teacher.

7. They appear very healthy.

8. She became a tutor after she retired from teaching.

9. Her kitchen always smells good.

10. Our neighborhood sounds noisy in the summer.

Write all of the linking verbs in alphabetical order on the lines below.

1. _____   4. _____   7. _____

2. _____   5. _____   8. _____

3. _____   6. _____   9. _____

10. _____

Try This! Circle all linking verbs in a magazine or newspaper article.

17   FS-30043 Grammar

At the Beach

Name _____

Remember: Some verbs show **action** while others **link** the subject to a word in the predicate which renames the subject or describes it.

Underline the action verbs and circle the linking verbs in the sentences below.

1. The day was warm and sunny.

2. The Nettler children were ready for the beach.

3. The children grew up in San Diego.

4. They grabbed their beach towels and headed for the jeep.

5. On the way, they stopped for sandwiches.

6. Mary was the first to hit the sand.

7. Helen appears to be the practical daughter.

8. She found a table for their lunch.

9. John and Tom became the carriers of
   the surfboards.

10. All four teenagers rode the waves before lunch.

11. Mother looks content reading her book
    about Harry Truman.

12. Hank built a fire for the barbecue.

13. Tom and John crashed into the waves often.

14. The girls became the best surfers that day.

15. The Nettlers stayed at the beach until the sun went down.

In the sentences containing linking verbs, draw an arrow from the subject to the word(s) that renames or describes it.

Example: Mary is the oldest child.

Working Together

Name _____

Helping verbs help the main verb. They come before the main verb. Some verbs cannot stand alone. They need helping verbs.

Below is a list of commonly used helping verbs.

have	shall	is	be	may
has	will	are	been	must
had	should	was	do	might
	would	were	did	
	could	am	does	

Underline the main verb and circle the helping verb in the sentences below.

1. The weather is turning cooler.

2. The holidays will be coming soon.

3. Chris is getting her house ready for the family.

4. Patrick and Michael might look for a tree tonight.

5. Kerry said, "I shall make the cookies."

6. "You should go to the store first," said Chris.

7. You may help me if you like.

8. They had been working in the kitchen most of the day.

9. Michael could drive the tree home in his pickup truck.

10. This should be a wonderful family celebration.

Try This! Open one of your textbooks. Write all the helping verbs from a page in the book.

Sailing Along

Name _____

Verbs are action words that sometimes need helping verbs. **Helping verbs** come before the main verb. **Linking verbs** show no action. They link the subject to the predicate.

Underline the verbs.
Write *MV* above the main verb.
Write *HV* above the helping verb.
Write *LV* above the linking verb.

1. Paul sailed his boat into the harbor.

2. He became a sailor at an early age.

3. He sure looks tan.

4. Mary has been cleaning the deck all day.

5. Mary and Betty brought their lunch in a large cooler.

6. Jim steered the sailboat out into the lake.

7. Pat was waving to the crew from the dock.

8. She should have gone with them.

9. The main sail was hard to raise.

10. Soon they were moving quickly through the water.

11. Sailing is relaxing.

Try This! Write three sentences, one containing each of the types of verbs, on the back of this sheet.

FS-30043 Grammar

Easy Does It!

Name _____

Some verbs show action. Some verbs do not show action, but they link the subject to a word in the predicate. Some verbs help verbs that cannot stand alone. They come before the main verb.

After each noun, write an action verb, a linking verb, or a helping verb with an action verb.

1. Bicycles _____ .

2. Students _____ .

3. Animals _____ .

4. Cities _____ .

5. Libraries _____ .

6. The audience _____ .

7. A doctor _____ .

8. Jets _____ .

Cross out the word in each line that is not a verb.

9.	poured	am	cat	came	skated
10.	appear	talked	has	table	dashed
11.	tastes	scissors	cut	be	is
12.	coat	dressed	was	looks	became
13.	sounds	drum	seems	has	trumpet
14.	been	feels	were	sat	wig
15.	being	have	jeep	do	grows
16.	smells	sleeps	carry	pencil	won

Try This! Write six sentences about your friends: two with action verbs, two with linking verbs, and two with helping verbs.

21

FS-30043 Grammar

Hit the Beach

Name _____

An **adjective** is a word used to describe a noun or pronoun.
An adjective tells **how many**, **what kind**, and **which ones**.

Make the paragraph below more interesting by writing an adjective on each line. Then, finish the story. Include ten adjectives in the ending.

It was _____ break. Mr. and

Mrs. Gramm were taking their

_____ family to a

_____ house on the Atlantic

Ocean. When they arrived, Paul took

_____, _____

suitcases into the house. The _____ daughter ran quickly down to the beach.

The rest of the _____ family changed into their swimsuits. A

_____ blanket, _____ chairs, a _____ umbrella, and

a _____ basket were dropped on the beach as the children raced into the

water. Carol jumped toward a _____ wave while Paul balanced with his

_____ board. "Be careful," shouted their _____ mother from the

shore. Mr. Gramm pulled up a _____, _____ chair and began

reading a _____ book about Egypt. At noon, they all gathered on the blanket

for a _____ lunch. The family continued to have a _____ time at

the beach until _____

_____

_____

Try This! Choose an article from a newspaper. Change the story by replacing existing adjectives in the story with new ones.

Get Moving

Name _____

Some **adjectives** are used to compare nouns. There are three forms of comparison—**positive**, **comparative**, and **superlative**.

The **positive** form describes a noun or pronoun without comparing it to anyone or anything else.

This is a _____ way to move.

1. quick   3. slow   5. tough

2. smooth   4. easy   6. cool

The **comparative** form (-er) compares two nouns.

Add *er* to the words above. Write them on the lines below.

_____

_____

1. _____   3. _____   5. _____

2. _____   4. _____   6. _____

The **superlative** form (-est) compares three or more nouns.

Add *est* to the words above. Write them on the lines below.

1. _____   3. _____   5. _____

2. _____   4. _____   6. _____

Try This! Write a story about your family using all three forms of comparison for three adjectives.

That's What Friends Are for!

Adjectives

and adverbs

Name _____

Adjectives and **adverbs** make the meaning of other words clearer and more specific. They modify. Adjectives modify nouns and pronouns. Adverbs modify verbs. They often end with *-ly*.

Example

Adjective	Adverb
The *early* bird gets the worm.	She rose *early* for school.

Write the correct word on the line and circle the word it modifies.

Jim and Pat planned a _____ party to surprise Helen on her birthday.
    fantastic, fantastically

On the day before the party, ten fourth-graders met _____ at Pat's house.
    secret, secretly

All morning, they _____ prepared food. They made cake, brownies, and
    quick, quickly

sticky _____ taffy. Then her friends went home and waited
    sweet, sweetly

_____ for the next day.
  excited, excitedly

At two o'clock, everyone arrived except Helen. An hour passed. The ice cream was

melting _____. Everyone was getting _____ . Jim said, "Let's
    slow, slowly   hungry, hungrily

call and see if she forgot!"

Helen answered the phone and was very _____ to find out that her
    happy, happily

friends were all waiting for her at a birthday party she was never invited to!

Try This! Using the newspaper, cut out five sentences containing adjectives and five containing adverbs. Attach them to the back of this page. Underline the adjectives and circle the adverbs.

© Frank Schaffer Publications, Inc.   24   FS-30043 Grammar

Three Plus Three

Name _____

An **adverb** is a word used to modify a verb, an adjective, or another adverb.
An adverb tells **how**, **when**, **where**, **why**, **how much**, and **how often**.

Circle the adverb in each sentence. Write on the line which question the adverb answers.

1. Our dog snores loudly. _____

2. He will begin digging the hole soon. _____

3. George quickly stacked the chairs in the truck. _____

4. Her temper is really explosive! _____

5. She sang beautifully at the concert. _____

6. We searched everywhere for the jewelry. _____

7. Peter always takes his bike on vacations. _____

8. Susan bathes daily. _____

9. Dad sings very loudly in the shower. _____

10. That student rarely misses school. _____

11. Leave your soccer uniform there. _____

12. Gently she picked up the baby. _____

13. Suddenly we saw the fireworks. _____

14. He works slowly but he never makes a mistake. _____

_____

15. Michelle said, "Let's go outside." _____

Try This!

On the back of this page, write the definition of an adverb. Write a news article relating to your school. Include five adverbs in it.

Up, Under, Around, and Through

Prepositions

Name _____

Prepositions show the relationship between a noun or a pronoun and another word in the sentence.

Examples
The boy *on* the skateboard flew by.
The girl *with* the magnifying glass studied the bug.
The rollerblades *under* the table are mine.

Some of the most common prepositions are:

about	among	below	down	inside	on	until
above	around	beside	for	into	over	up
across	at	beyond	from	near	to	with
after	before	by	in	of	under	without

Prepositions are usually found in phrases. A **prepositional phrase** is a group of words that begins with a preposition and ends with a noun.

Using the three sentences in the examples above, write each prepositional phrase on the line and circle the preposition.

1. _____

2. _____

3. _____

Complete the prepositional phrases below by writing a noun on the line and circling the preposition.

4. with the _____

5. beside a _____

6. near the huge _____

7. under the _____

8. above a _____

9. around the smooth_____

Try This! On the back of this paper, write five sentences containing prepositional phrases. Underline the phrase and circle the preposition.

© Frank Schaffer Publications, Inc.

26

FS-30043 Grammar

Hit the Target!

Name _____

Prepositions show the relationship between a noun or pronoun and another word in the sentence. A preposition never stands alone. It needs an object.

 Example   The dog is <u>under the table</u>.

Underline the prepositional phrase(s) in each sentence below.
Draw an arrow from the preposition to its object.

1. The book was written by a person named A. Adams.

2. The story was about a Missouri family.

3. They went across the street for ice cream.

4. Will you stay after school to help with the play?

5. Doing without breakfast will lead to poor health.

6. You must stay within the area of the schoolyard.

7. Work until it gets dark.

8. Tracy was on the basketball team.

9. Doug got inside the tent.

10. The pizza party was for the whole class.

Write a paragraph about your school containing ten prepositional phrases. Give it to a classmate and have him or her circle all the prepositions.

 **Try This!**   On the back of this page, tape a paragraph from the sports section of the newspaper. Circle all the prepositions it contains.

27

Bridging the Gap

Name _____

Conjunctions join together words, phrases, or clauses.

> **Example** ▶ Michelle *and* James
> after school *but* before dinner
> My mother brings me to school *since* I cannot drive.

The most common conjunctions are:

and	or	but
for	either…or	neither…nor
of	although	since
in order that	as	because
unless	after	before
until	when	where
while	however	therefore

Circle the conjunction in each sentence below. Underline the words, phrases, or clauses that have been joined by the conjunction.

1. Sarah and Elizabeth went skating at Ballwin Skating Rink.

2. To get to the skating rink, you must go over the bridge and through the gate.

3. Peter likes to ice skate, but he would rather go inline skating on the sidewalks in the park.

4. Jim went to Forest Park where he saw Peter.

5. Skateboarding and rollerblading are both fun.

6. The day was sunny although there were clouds in the sky.

7. We could have lunch at McDonald's unless you want to come to my house.

8. I need to go home now, besides, my feet are killing me.

Try This!   On the back of this page, write three sentences about your favorite sport. Use a conjunction in each sentence.

More Alike Than Different

Name _____

A **conjunction** joins together words, phrases, or clauses.

Complete the sentences below with an appropriate conjunction.

1. Jennifer _____ Anne have been friends since kindergarten.

2. Walk to school _____ take your bike.

3. Nick is slow _____ his work is perfect every time.

4. _____ clean your room _____ take out the trash.

5. Get outside today _____ tomorrow it may rain.

6. Lift the weights over your head, _____ you think you can.

7. William was in the basement _____ the lights went out.

8. Go with your dad _____ you would like to wait for me.

9. You have finished your homework _____ you may watch TV.

10. Father began to whistle _____ he was happy.

Try This!

On the back of this page, write a paragraph about winter using these conjunctions: *neither...nor, in order that,* and *since.*

FS-30043 Grammar

Wow!

Name _____

Interjections are words or groups of words that express strong feelings. Interjections are followed by exclamation points.

Circle the interjections in the sentences below.

1. "Bravo!" yelled the crowd in the stadium.

2. Wow! What a catch.

3. The coach said, "Terrific! That was a great play."

4. "Well! Well! Our opponents looked depressed," said the quarterback.

5. Hurry! Get back on the field.

6. My! My! The fans gave us a standing ovation.

7. Nonsense! They were just tired from sitting so long.

8. Hey! Let's celebrate.

Listen carefully to your friends, teachers, and other school staff during lunch and recess. Write down any interjections you hear spoken.

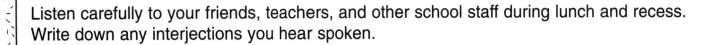

_____

_____

_____

_____

_____

Try This! Write a dialogue between you and a friend about a sports event. Include ten interjections.

Answers

Page 2
1. Peter   2. malt
3. Peter   4. Peter
5. woman   6. She
7. name   8. Michelle
9. rollerblades   10. Bike riding
11. San Diego   12. boys
13. man   14. Mr. Farmer
15. Jogging

Page 3
1. is his best friend
2. have computers at home
3. drove her van to school
4. goes to that newly built school
5. takes computer classes after school
6. is horseback riding
7. was not very hard for him
8. takes dancing lessons on Saturdays
9. worked on their science project together
10. teaches fourth grade at Washington Elementary School

1. drove   2. goes
3. have   4. is
5. is   6. takes
7. takes   8. teaches
9. was   10. worked

Page 4
1. we / go
2. school / has
3. Everyone / will
4. Hanukkah / is
5. tree / was
6. I / would
7. father / gave
8. Megan / led
9. Hunt / is
10. family / celebrates
11. Peter / were
12. school / will
13. July / is
14. St. Louis / is

Page 5
Answers will vary.
Page 6
Answers will vary.

Page 7
verb, pronoun, adverb, interjection, preposition, adjective, conjunction, noun

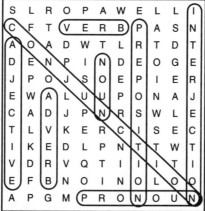

Page 8
2.-5. Answers will vary.
6. people, Vietnam War
7. statue, Lincoln
8. George Washington, city

Page 9
1. Barbara (p), basketball (c), backboard (c)
2. Carl (p), cold (c), Canada (p)
3. Dorothy (p), dancing (c)
4. Easter (p), Eugene (p), eggs (c)
5. Frank (p), face (c), Frances (p)
6. George (p), Gracie (p), goose (c), graduation (c)
7. hamburgers (c), home (c)
8. ice cream (c), indigestion (c), in-laws (c)
9. Justin (p), jellybeans (c), jacket (c)
10. Karen (p), kindergarten (c), kangaroo (c)
11. Lucy (p), laughs (c), line (c)
12. mouths (c), memories (c)
13. Nancy (p), Norman (p), neck (c)
14. outings (c), Otto (p), oranges (c), officers (c)
15. Patricia (p), Paul (p), porch (c)
16. Quentin (p), quilt (c)

Page 10
Answers will vary.

Page 11
1. Angie's computer
2. doctor's stethoscope
3. farmer's land
4. artist's painting
5. teacher's pupils
6. catcher's mitt
7. astronaut's name
8. lake's water

9. Kathy's horse
10. Mr. Lincoln's hat

Page 12
Answers will vary.

Page 13
The following pronouns should be replaced:
1. He   2. It   3. she
4. It   5. They   6. we
7. it   8. them   9. Mine
10. hers   11. us   12. theirs
13. Yours   14. Its   15. us

Page 14
1. There   2. their
3. Their   4. there
5. their, there   6. There
7. Their   8. there
9. their, there   10. there
11. Their, there   12. there, their
13. there

Page 15
was, was, teethed, played, <u>could have grown up</u>, felt, <u>was getting</u>, loaded, started, moved, drove, got, <u>started bugging</u>, <u>were going at it</u>, <u>could have turned</u>, <u>fell out</u>, landed, <u>had been fighting</u>, <u>didn't notice</u>, pulled, sat, watching, <u>walk up</u>, sniff, said, knew, thought, <u>had found</u>, picked, carried

Page 16

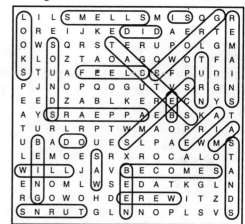

Page 17
1. Joe <u>is</u> a neighbor.
2. He usually <u>seems</u> happy.
3. I <u>am</u> pleased.
4. Joe <u>became</u> a boxer.

31

5. Karen <u>is</u> his wife.

6. She <u>was</u> a teacher.

7. They <u>appear</u> very healthy.

8. She <u>became</u> a tutor…

9. Her kitchen always <u>smells</u> good.

10. Our neighborhood <u>sounds</u> noisy…

Alphabetical Order
1. am
2. appear
3. became
4. became
5. is
6. is
7. seems
8. smells
9. sounds
10. was

Page 18
1. was-LV
2. were-LV
3. grew up-AV
4. grabbed, headed-AV
5. stopped-AV
6. was-LV, hit-AV
7. appears-LV
8. found-AV
9. became-LV
10. rode-AV
11. looks-LV, reading-AV
12. built-AV
13. crashed-AV
14. became-LV
15. stayed-AV, went-LV

Page 19
Main verb is underlined. Helping verb is in boldfaced type.
1. **is** <u>turning</u>
2. **will be** <u>coming</u>
3. **is** <u>getting</u>
4. **might** <u>look</u>
5. **shall** <u>make</u>
6. **should** <u>go</u>
7. **may** <u>help</u>
8 **had been** <u>working</u>
9. **could** <u>drive</u>
10. **should** <u>be</u>

Page 20
1. sailed-MV
2. became-LV
3. looks-LV
4. has been-HV, cleaning-MV
5. brought-MV

6. steered-MV
7. was-HV, waving-MV
8. should have-HV, gone MV
9. was-LV
10. were-HV, moving-MV
11. is-LV

Page 21
1.-8. Answers will vary.
9. cat
10. table
11. scissors
12. coat
13. trumpet
14. wig
15. jeep
16. pencil

Page 22
Answers will vary.

Page 23
Comparative:
1. quicker
2. smoother
3. slower
4. easier
5. tougher
6. cooler

Superlative:
1. quickest
2. smoothest
3. slowest
4. easiest
5. toughest
6. coolest

Page 24
Modified words are in boldfaced type.
1. fantastic; **party**
2. secretly; **met**
3. quickly; **prepared**
4. sweet; **taffy**
5. excitedly; **waited**
6. slowly; **melting**
7. hungry; **everyone**
8. happy; **Helen**

Page 25
1. loudly-how
2. soon-when
3. quickly-how
4. really-how
5. beautifully-how
6. everywhere-where
7. always-when or how often
8. daily-how often or when
9. loudly-how
10. rarely-when or how often
11. there-where
12. Gently-how
13. Suddenly-how or when
14. slowly-how; never-when or how often
15. outside-where

Page 26
Prepositions are in boldfaced type.
1. **on** the skateboard
2. **with** the magnifying glass
3. **under** the table

4.-9.—Nouns will vary. Prepositions:
4. with
5. beside
6. near
7. under
8. above
9. around

Page 27
1. by a person
2. about a Missouri family
3. across the street, for ice cream
4. after school, with the play
5. without breakfast, to poor health
6. within the area, of the schoolyard
7. until it gets dark
8. on the basketball team
9. inside the tent
10. for the whole class

Page 28
Conjunctions are in boldfaced type.
1. Sarah **and** Elizabeth
2. over the bridge **and** through the gate
3. Underline entire sentence, circle **but**.
4. Underline entire sentence, circle **where**.
5. Skateboarding **and** rollerblading
6. Underline entire sentence, circle **although**.
7. Underline entire sentence, circle **unless**.
8. Underline entire sentence, circle **besides**.

Page 29
Answers will vary.

Page 30
1. Bravo!
2. Wow!
3. Terrific!
4. Well! Well!
5. Hurry!
6. My! My!
7. Nonsense!
8. Hey!